learn to draw
Planes, Choppers & Watercraft

Learn to draw 22 different subjects,
step by easy step,
shape by simple shape!

Illustrated by Tom LaPadula

Associate Publisher: Elizabeth T. Gilbert
Art Director: Shelley Baugh
Managing Editor: Rebecca J. Razo
Associate Editor: Emily Green
Production Artists: Debbie Aiken, Rae Siebels

www.walterfoster.com
Walter Foster Publishing, Inc.
3 Wrigley, Suite A
Irvine, CA 92618

1 3 5 7 9 10 8 6 4 2

Table of Contents

Getting Started

When you look closely at the drawings in this book, you'll notice that they're made up of basic shapes, such as circles, ovals, and triangles. To draw the high-powered moving machines in this book, just start with simple shapes as you see here. It's easy and fun!

Rectangles
are one way to start a heavy-duty cargo ship.

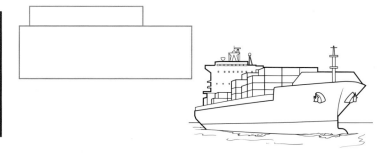

Ovals
are great for the body of a helicopter.

Triangles
are perfect for the wings of a jet plane.

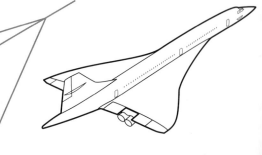

Tools & Materials

Before you begin, gather some drawing tools, such as paper, a regular pencil, an eraser, and a pencil sharpener. For color, you can use markers, colored pencils, paint, crayons, or even colored chalk.

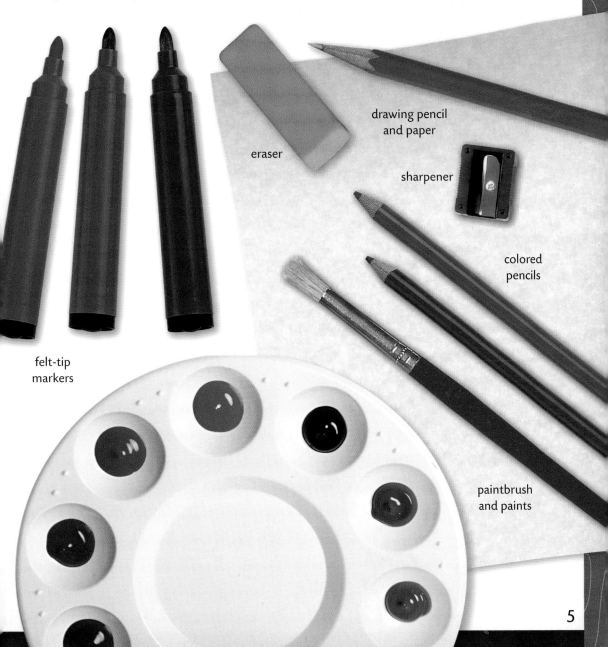

drawing pencil
and paper

eraser

sharpener

colored
pencils

felt-tip
markers

paintbrush
and paints

Twin-Engine Aircraft

This sleek, angular aircraft sports six seats
and wingtip-mounted fuel tanks.

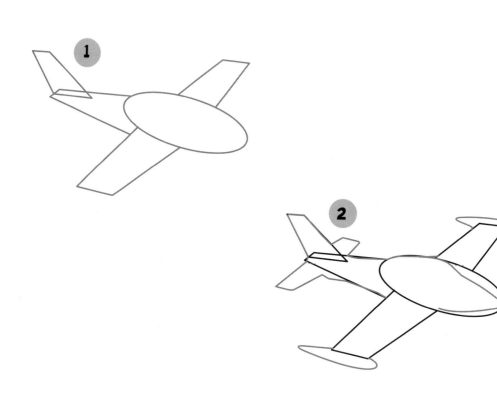

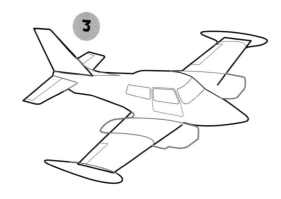

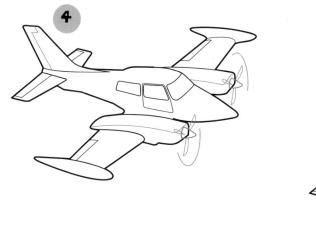

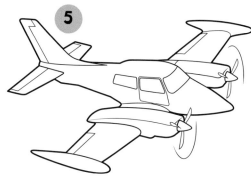

Fun Fact

This airplane can land on a tundra in Alaska or in the wild Australian Outback. Special equipment allows the plane to land in remote areas without a normal runway—while carrying up to 2,000 pounds of cargo!

Single-Engine Aircraft

This compact fixed-wing plane seats four, including the pilot, and it only costs $300,000—pocket change!

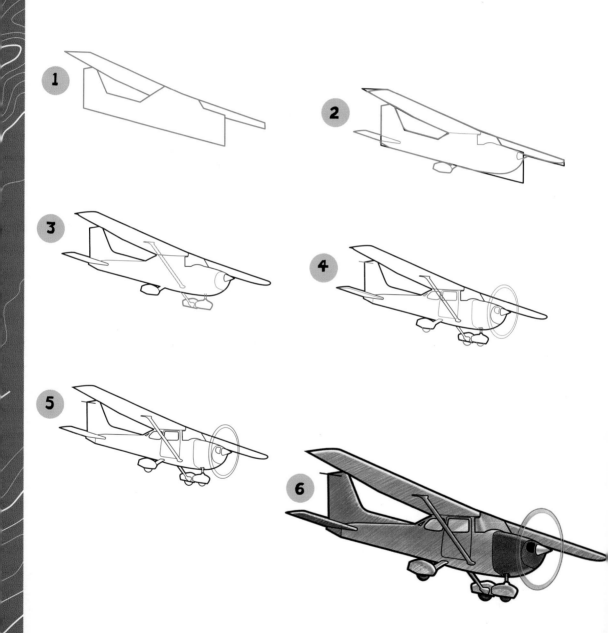

Tandem-Rotor Helicopter

This beast can seat **44** people and carry up to **20,000** pounds: enough load capacity to lift another helicopter!

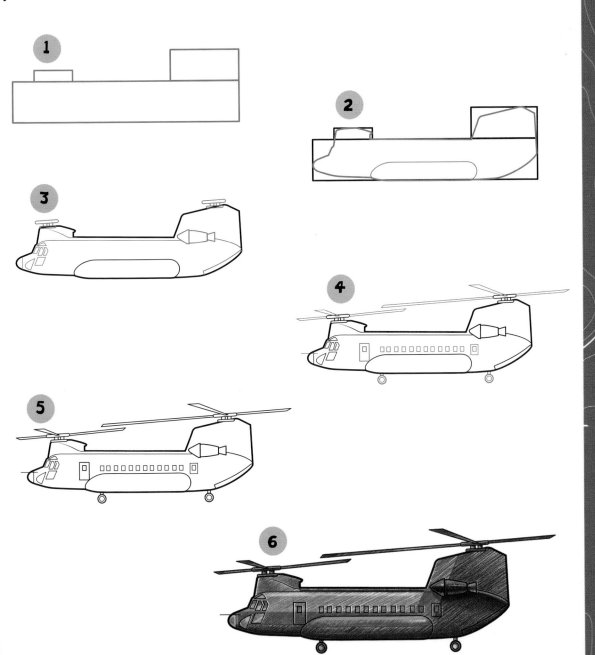

Cargo Ship

Powered by a diesel engine, this massive vessel transports cargo to shipping ports all over the world.

1
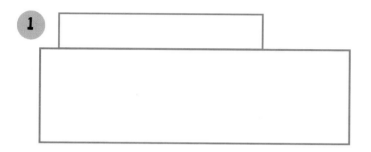

2
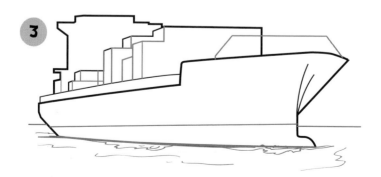

3
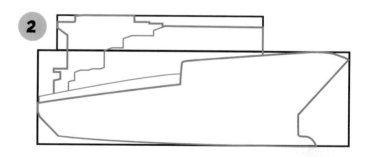

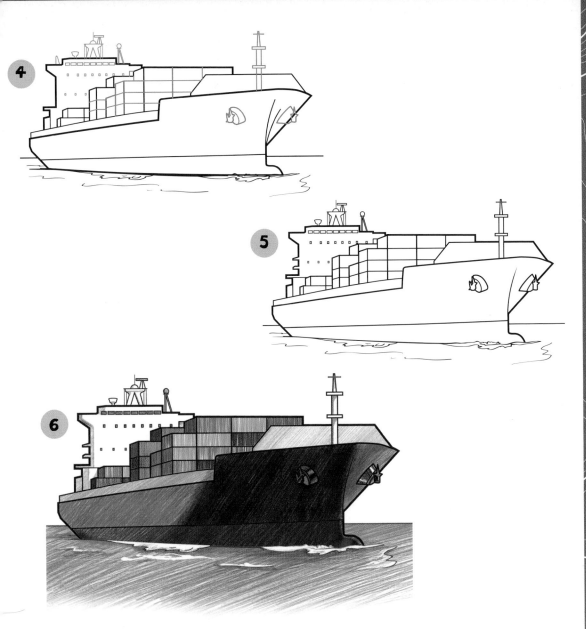

Fun Fact

Cargo ships carry goods in large steel containers stacked on top of each other—as many as 15,000 containers stacked 60 feet above deck! Giant cranes move the containers on and off the ships; then they place them onto trains and semi-trucks to travel to their land destinations.

Twin-Propeller Airliner

Manufactured from 1934 to 1937, this aluminum plane could seat 14 people and travel 1,000 miles in one trip.

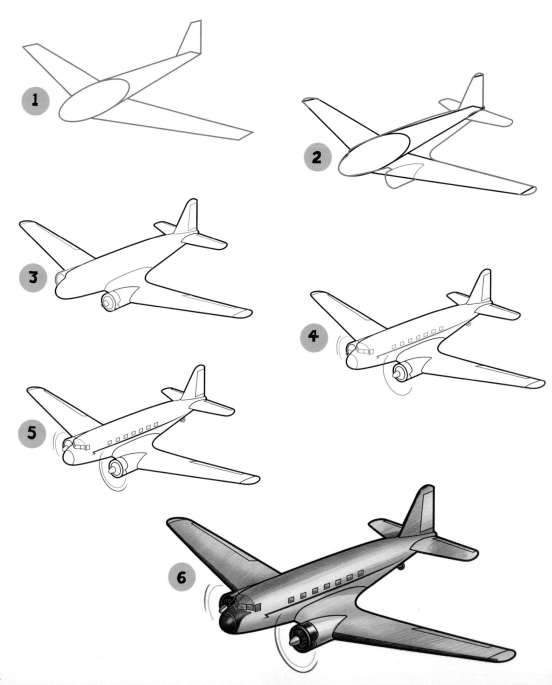

Three-Engine Wide-Body Aircraft

This airplane was manufactured from 1971 to 1989. It could seat 380 people and fly up to 610 miles per hour.

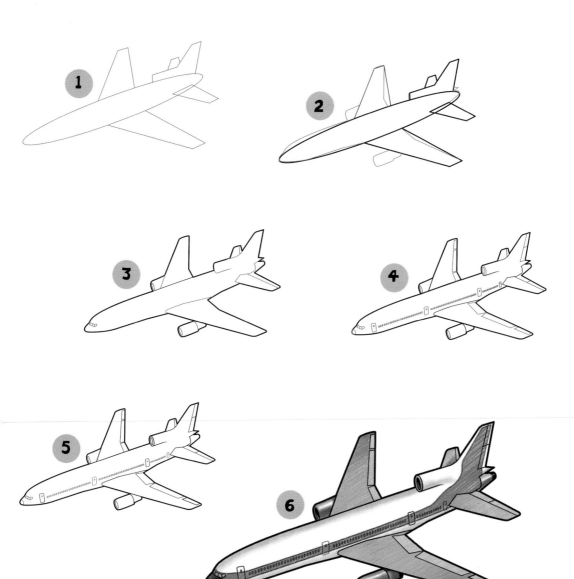

Search and Rescue (SAR) Helicopter

This chopper sports a watertight hull, allowing it to land on water. It is frequently used to rescue people at sea.

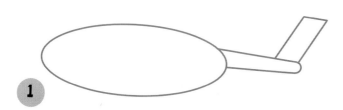

1

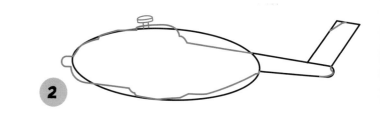

2

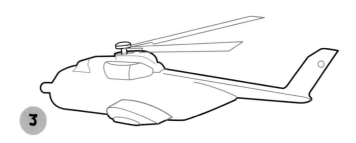

3

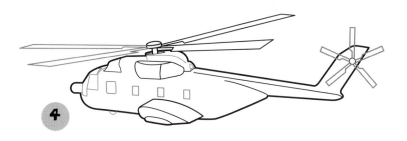

4

5

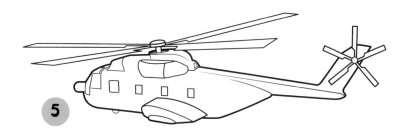

6

Fun Fact

In 1967, two of these tough choppers completed the first nonstop helicopter trip across the Atlantic Ocean. They took off from New York and landed in Paris 30 hours later—but they were refueled nine times while in the air!

Tugboat

This tough little boat packs a lot of power. It can push or pull cargo ships into and out of crowded canals.

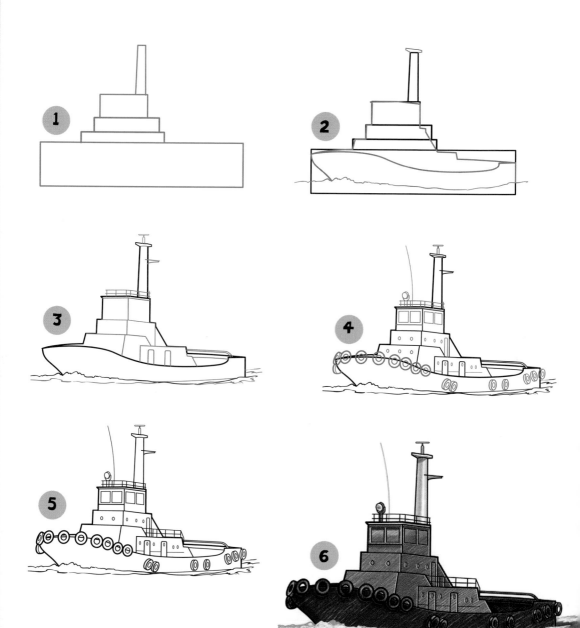

Supersonic Airliner

This plane flies **60,000** feet above sea level.
Triangular wings and turbo engines help it travel
twice the speed of most other planes.

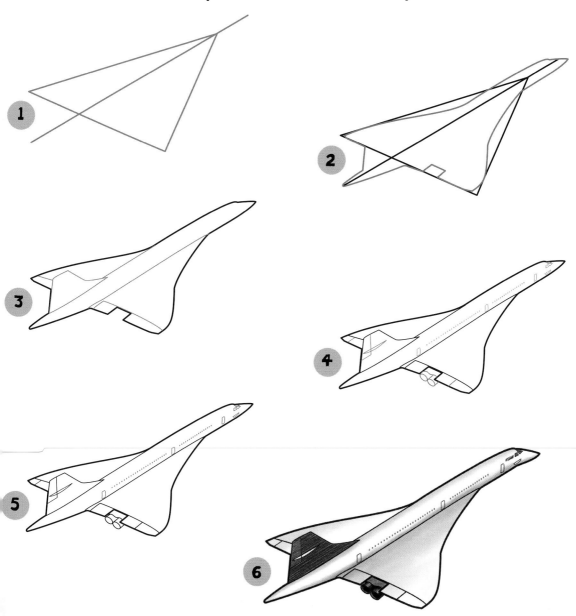

Riverboat

This boat uses steam power and large paddles to operate. A flat bottom helps it steer in shallow water.

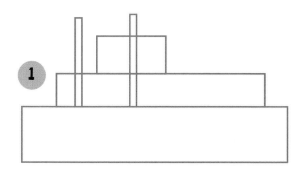

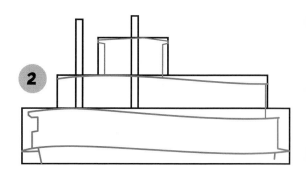

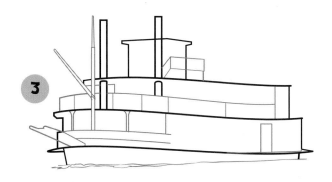

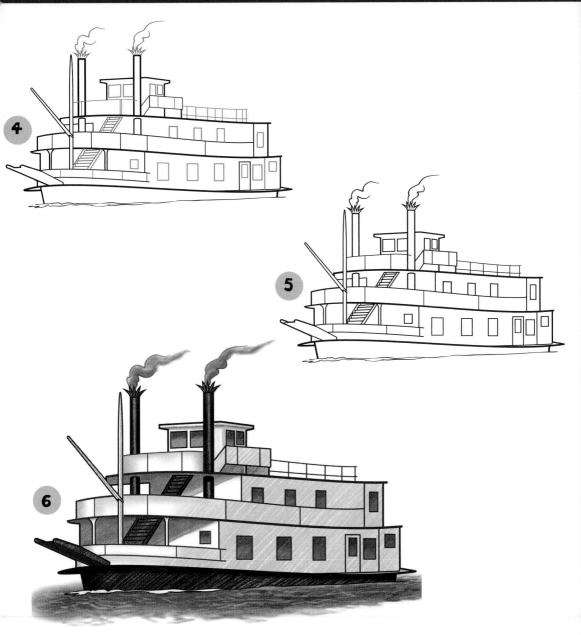

4

5

6

Fun Fact

In the late 1800s, Mark Twain piloted a riverboat and wrote about his experiences in a book called *Life on the Mississippi.* There are few riverboats on the Mississippi River today; their engines often exploded, so most were destroyed.

Light Aerobatic Biplane

This plane can perform tricks, including spinning in a roll, looping in a figure 8, and flying upside down!

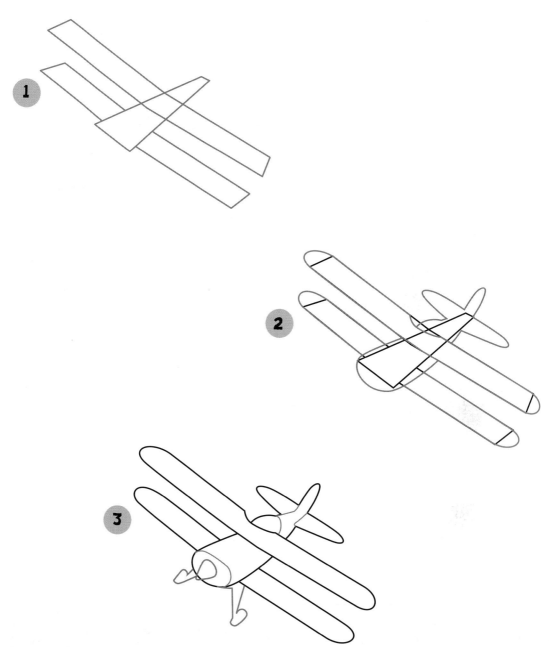

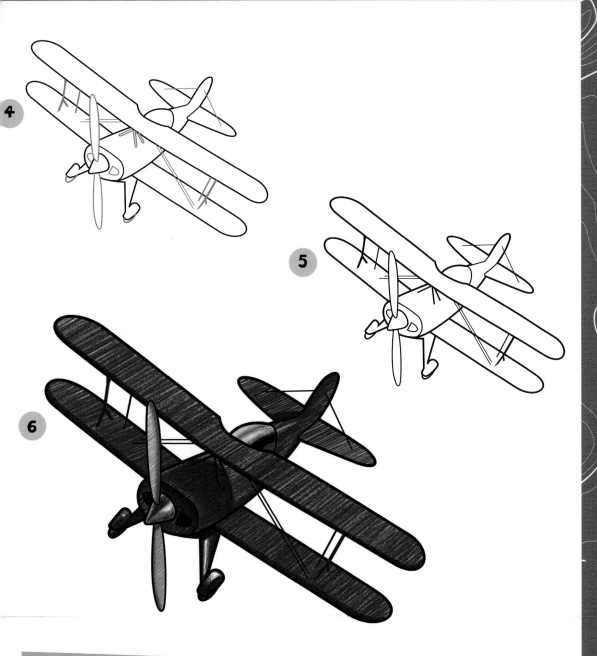

Fun Fact

Since 1944, this double-winged plane has won hundreds of aerobatic competitions around the world. Adventurous pilots are so proud of their speedy machines that they decorate them in fancy designs and colors.

Hovercraft

This rectangular craft can jet across ice, snow, and water. It uses high-speed fans to create an air cushion underneath its rubber sides—it literally floats on air!

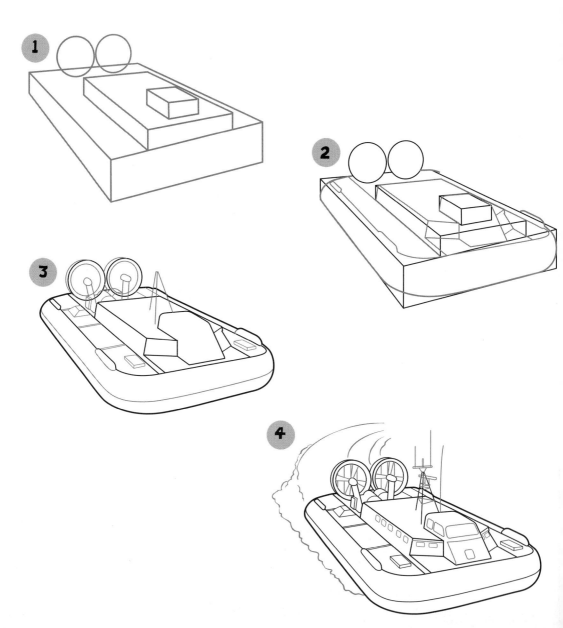

5

6

Fun Fact

Hovercrafts can easily float over mud, so they are often used in rescue operations to help save people trapped in flooded areas.

Jumbo Jet

This double-decker aircraft has four engines. It can carry 500 people and travel 8,000 miles in one trip.

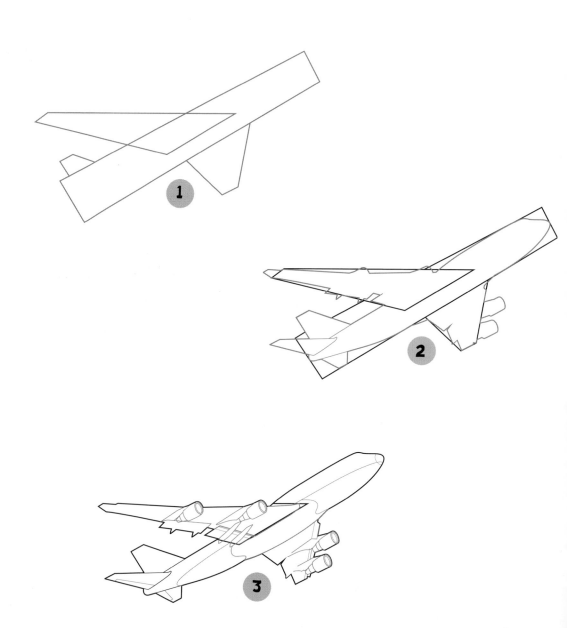

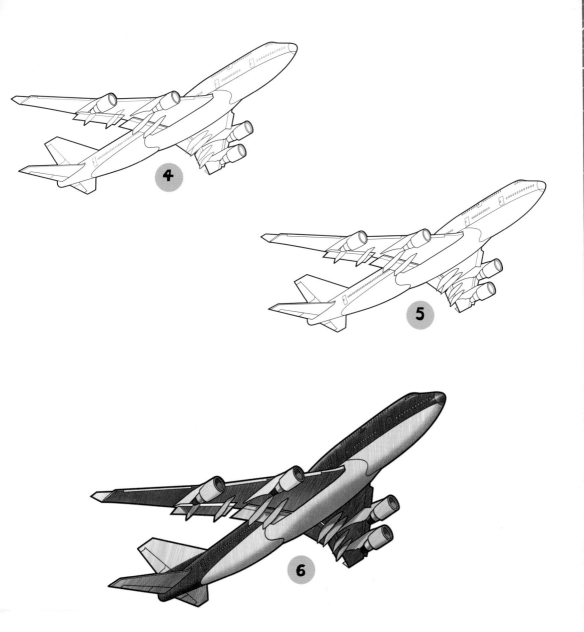

Fun Fact

This jumbo jet is so gigantic that its manufacturer had to build a special factory for it. It has its own special airplane that flies big pieces of the jet to the production plant.

All-Metal Twin-Engine Aircraft

This eight-seat, six-passenger plane was manufactured from 1936 to 1941, but it still flies on occasion today.

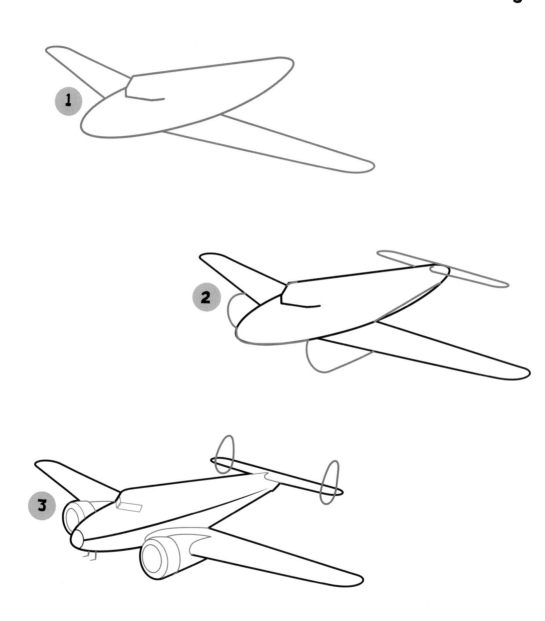

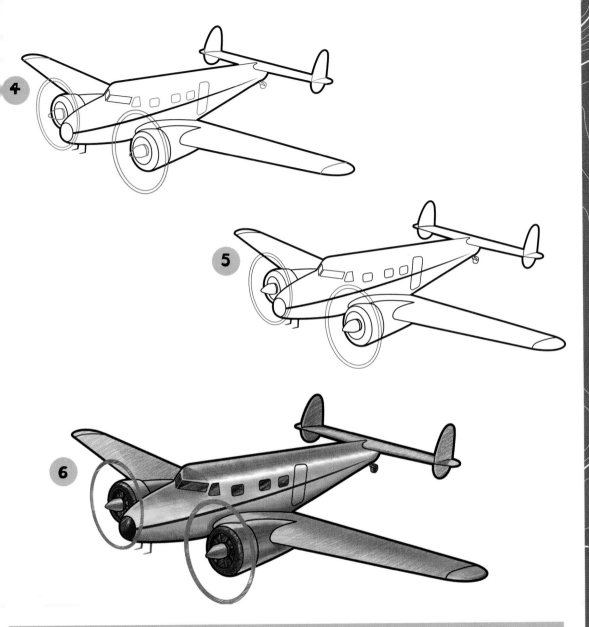

Fun Fact

Early engineers used these sturdy planes to test "de-icing" technology. De-icing removes ice that has frozen onto a plane's wings by using the aircraft's engine exhaust gas to melt the ice.

Polar Research Vessel

This powerful ship rams through ice up to 6 feet thick!
Its steel hull acts like a sledgehammer, floating up onto
ice and crushing it with a 13,000-ton weight.

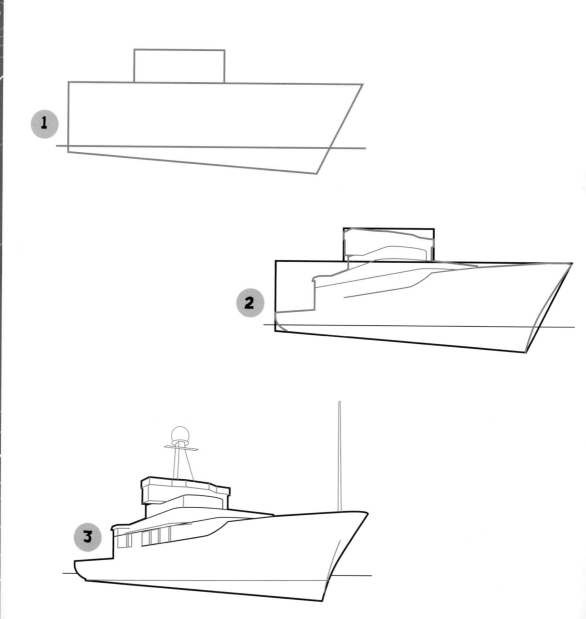

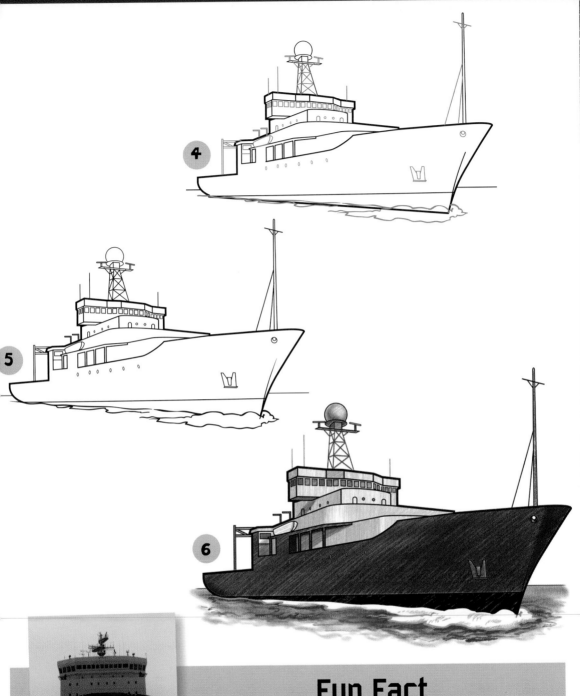

Fun Fact

Early polar research vessels were built of wood with bands of iron wrapped around their hulls to break ice. Later, steam-powered versions used paddles to crush the frozen waters. Modern versions run on multiple gas and diesel-electric engines, and some even use nuclear reactors!

Wright Flyer

The Wright Flyer was the world's first airplane. It was invented in 1903 by the famous Wright Brothers.

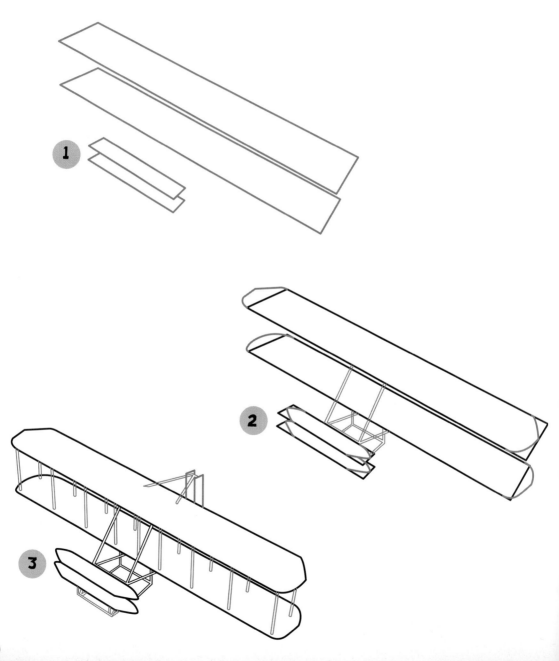

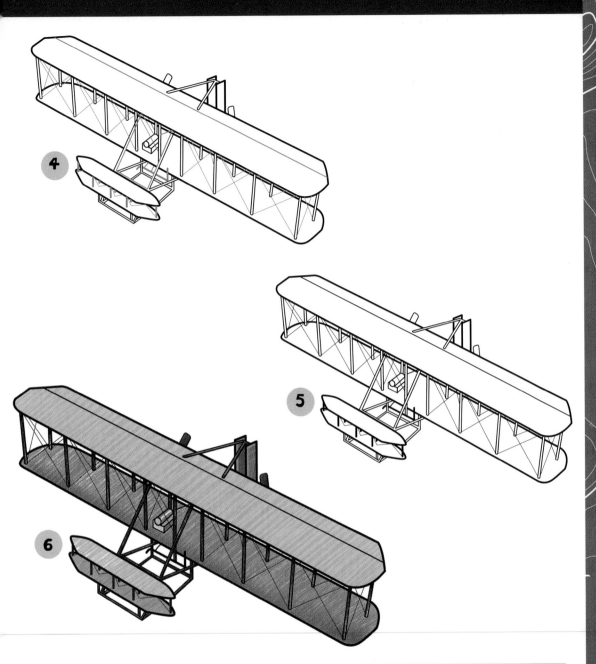

4

5

6

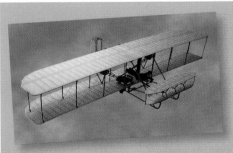

Fun Fact

The Wright Brothers flew their plane by lying on their stomachs and using their hips to direct the wings. They also used wires and a wooden lever to steer!

Ocean Steamer

This huge ship runs on steam. Wood or coal burns inside furnaces, heating large boilers filled with water. This, in turn, produces the steam that moves the engines.

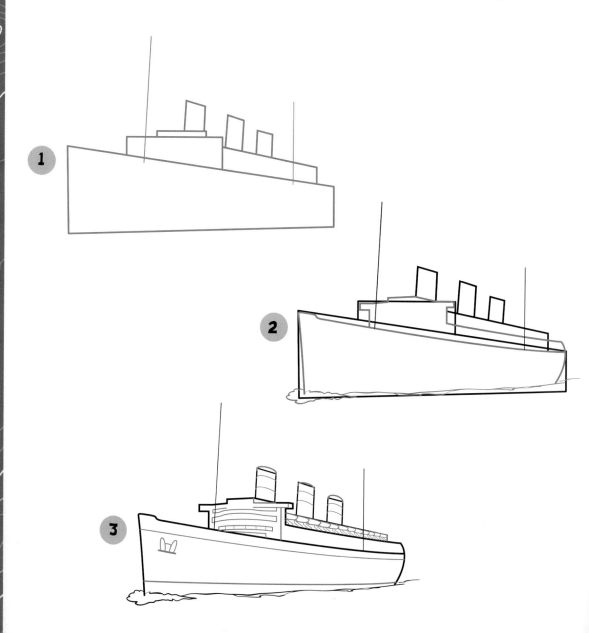

4

5

6

Medium-Lift Transport Helicopter

This twin-engine chopper can be modified to perform many different tasks, including helping to fight fires!

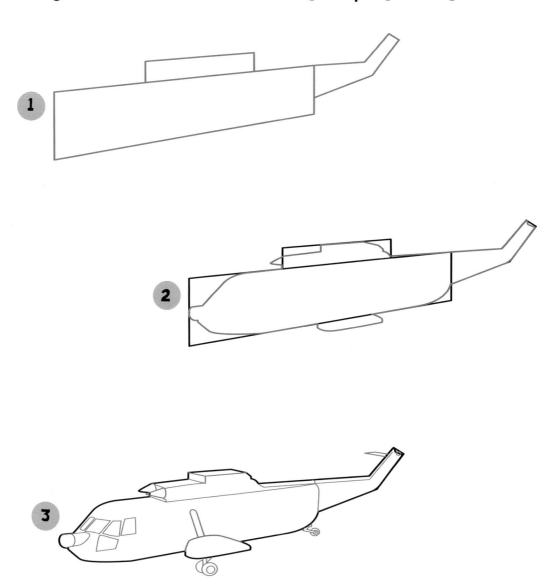

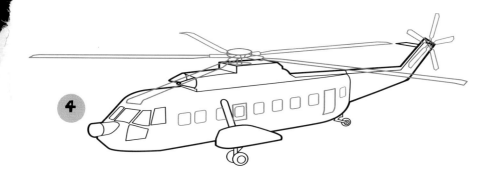

4

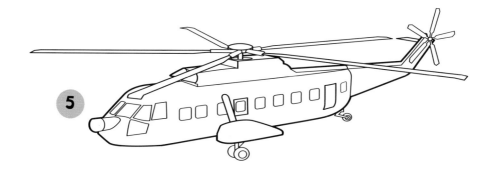

5

6

Short Take-Off and Landing Aircraft

First manufactured in 1951, this plane is capable of landing on both snow and water.

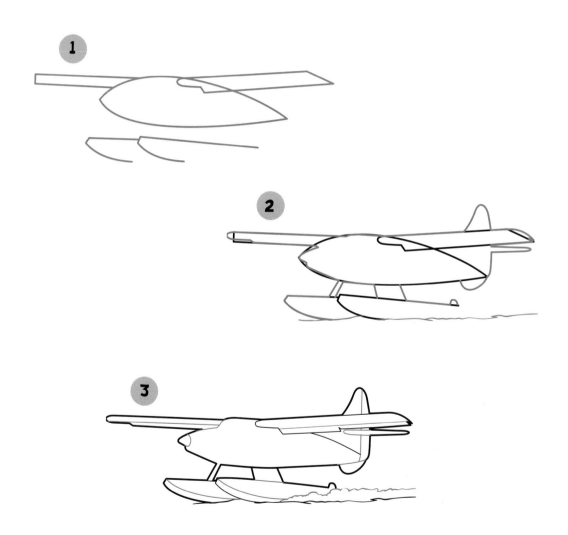

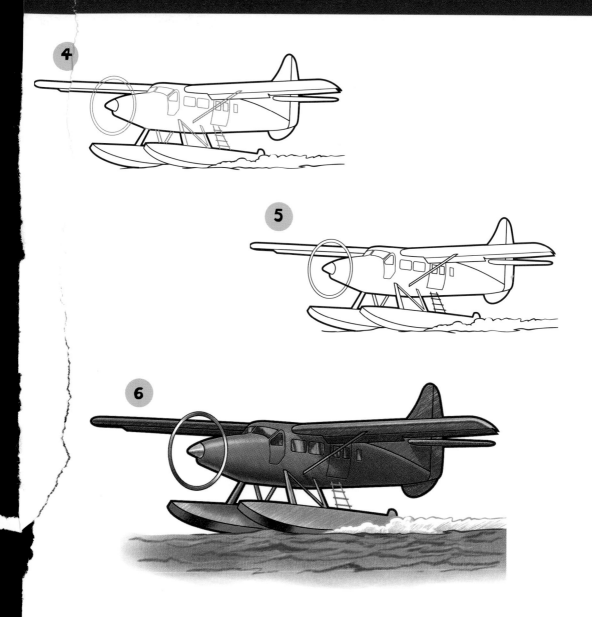

Fun Fact

There are different variations of this aircraft, which is sometimes called the "Otter" or the "King Beaver." Early versions of this easy-to-maneuver plane helped explorers map the Antarctic and Alaska!

Lightweight Twin-Engine Multipurpose Helicopter

This sharp-looking chopper seats six passengers and two pilots. Its fast engine can even overtake speedboats.

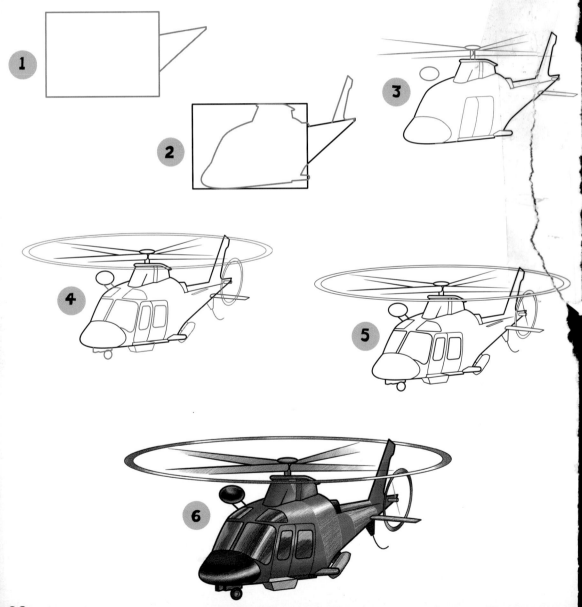

Light Utility Helicopter

This chopper is very quiet thanks to its covered tail rotor. Giant windows offer passengers a wonderful view.

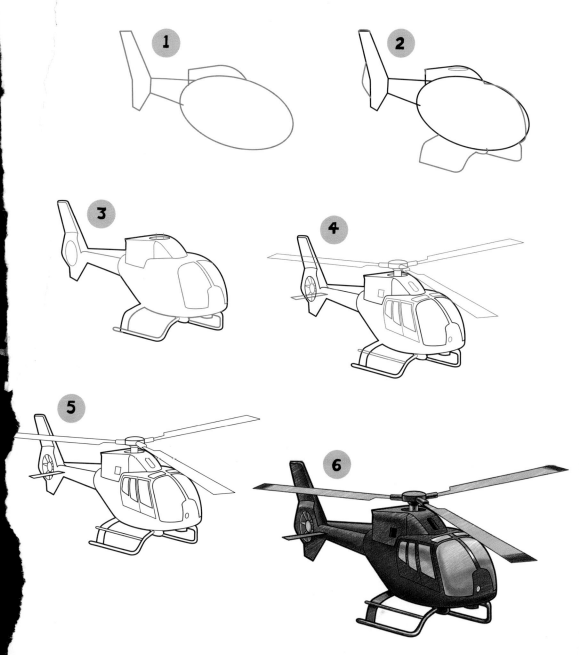

Single-Engine Light Aircraft

This aircraft was one of the first single-engine planes with a fully pressurized cabin that allowed passengers to breathe comfortably 10,000 feet above sea level.

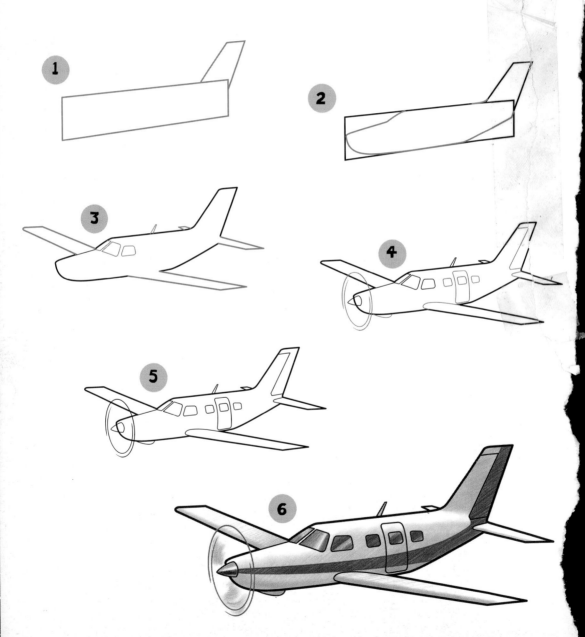